MW00934736

This Journal Belongs To

____

____

Made in the USA
Monee, IL
13 March 2021

62636024R00073